A CourseGuide for

Saving Truth

Abdu Murray

ZONDERVAN
REFLECTIVE

ZONDERVAN REFLECTIVE

A CourseGuide for Saving Truth

Copyright © 2019 by Zondervan

Requests for information should be addressed to:
Zondervan, *3900 Sparks Dr. SE, Grand Rapids, Michigan 49546*

ISBN 978-0-310-11120-7 (softcover)

Printed in the United States of America

CONTENTS

Introduction

Welcome to *A CourseGuide for Saving Truth*. These guides were created for formal and informal students alike who want to engage deeper in biblical, theological, or ministry studies. We hope this guide will provide an opportunity for you to grow not only in your understanding, but also in your faith.

How to Use this Guide

This guide is meant to be used in conjunction with the book *Saving Truth* and its corresponding videos, *Saving Truth Video Study*. After you have read each chapter in the book and watched the accompanying video lesson, the materials in this guide will help you review and assess what you have learned. Application-oriented questions are included as well. For additional practice, you will want to complete exercises found in *Saving Truth Study Guide*.

Each CourseGuide has been individually designed to best equip you in your studies, but in general, you can expect the following components. Most CourseGuides begin every chapter with a "You Should Know" section, which highlights key terminology, people, and facts to remember. This section serves as a helpful summary for directing your studies. Reflection questions, typically two to three per chapter, prompt you to summarize key points you've learned. Discussion questions invite you to an even deeper level of engagement. Finally, most chapters will end with a short quiz to test your retention. You can find the answer key to each quiz at the bottom of the page following it.

For Further Study

CourseGuides accompany books and videos from some of the world's top biblical and theological scholars. They may be used independently, or in small groups or classrooms, offering quality instruction to equip students for academic and ministry pursuits. If you would like to engage in further study with Zondervan's CourseGuides, the full lineup may be viewed online. After completing your studies with *A CourseGuide for Saving Truth*, we recommend moving on to *A CourseGuide for Tactics*, *A CourseGuide for Know Why You Believe*, and *A CourseGuide for Apologetics at the Cross*.

CHAPTER 1

The Blossoming of the Culture of Confusion

You Should Know

- Post-truth: denoting circumstances in which objective facts are less influential in shaping public opinion than appeals to emotion and personal belief

- Postmodernism: a worldview that tries to reject objective truth

- Examples of soft post-truth: an individual feels offended when they are told they are not the gender they claim to be; a Universalist claims that all paths lead to God

- Examples of hard post-truth: a Christian posts an article on Facebook, claiming a scientist lied about something, but after discovering the scientist did not lie, continues to post about how this scientist cannot be trusted; a politician promises greater freedom for people if he is elected, but actually desires to put greater restraints on their freedom

- Cynic: someone who will not believe a truth claim even if there is sufficient evidence

- Skeptic: someone who will not believe a truth claim unless there is sufficient evidence

- In the post-truth culture, facts are often perceived as a problem to get around instead of useful tools to use.

Reflection Questions

1. What is the difference between postmodernism and post-truth?

2. How can personal feelings end up subordinating truth?

3. How is Pilate an example of one who followed post-truth?

Discussion Question

1. If you were giving an account for the hope you had within you, how would you respond to someone who said, "That might be true for you, but that is not true for me"?

Quiz

1. What does "post-truth" mean?
   a) Denoting circumstances in which objective facts are less influential in shaping public opinion than appeals to emotion and personal belief
   b) Denoting circumstances in which subjective facts are less influential in shaping public opinion than appeal to emotion and personal belief
   c) Denoting circumstances in which objective facts are more influential in shaping public opinion than appeal to emotion and personal belief
   d) None of the above

2. According to Murray, soft post-truth suggests:
   a) Objective truth does not exist
   b) Objective truth exists, but feelings and opinions matter more
   c) A blatant falsehood is promoted, knowing it is false
   d) A blatant falsehood is promoted in ignorance of the fact that it is false

3. According to Murray, hard post-truth suggests:
   a) Objective truth does not exist
   b) Objective truth exists, but feelings and opinions matter more
   c) A blatant falsehood is promoted, knowing it is false
   d) A blatant falsehood is promoted in ignorance of the fact that it is false

4. Simply put, what was postmodernism's defining goal?

    a) The rejection of objective truth
    b) The rejection of modern philosophy
    c) The acceptance of modern ethics
    d) The embracing of an all-encompassing norm for understanding the world

5. What area is immune to the influence of post-truth?

    a) The church
    b) The culture
    c) Education
    d) None of the above

6. In a post-truth context, people look for:

    a) Editorialized facts to support their preferences
    b) Truth wherever it may be found
    c) Facts
    d) All of the above

7. A skeptic will not believe a truth claim:

    a) Unless an authority makes the claim
    b) Even if an authority makes the claim
    c) Unless there is sufficient evidence
    d) Even if there is sufficient evidence

8. A cynic will not believe a truth claim:

    a) Unless an authority makes the claim
    b) Even if an authority makes the claim
    c) Unless there is sufficient evidence
    d) Even if there is sufficient evidence

9. According to Murray, what was Pontius Pilate's error in interacting with Jesus?

    a) He did not listen to his wife
    b) He thought Jesus might be guilty, but he could not prove it
    c) He subordinated truth to his personal preference
    d) None of the above

10. Murray suggests the snare of post-truth is:
    a) It is not hard to find truth, but it is hard to embrace
    b) It is hard to find truth, but once found, it is easy to embrace
    c) It is hard to find truth and then embrace it
    d) It makes an individual incapable of reasoning

CHAPTER 2

Confusion and the Church: Seductions of a Post-Truth Mind

You Should Know

- We treat with dignity people we disagree with by: 1) acknowledging our own sins before them; 2) looking at the person as having been made in the image of God; and 3) praying for them.

- Examples of disagreeing in an agreeable manner: expressing that the gospel is needed by a sinner you are speaking with after honestly acknowledging that you are a sinner; listening to the difficulties of someone struggling with gender issues while waiting to proclaim the healing power of Jesus; acknowledging and commending the good intentions of a policy we disagree with; listening patiently to charges against our ideas and seeking to understand where those charges are coming from before answering them.

- Do not judge, lest you be judged: Jesus's warning that when we judge, it should be to improve someone rather than condemn them

- Pharisee: religious leader of Jesus's day who sought to love God's law, but did so at the expense of loving the people around them

- Integrity: honoring of truth and maintaining the dignity of others

- In but not of the culture: engaging with the culture but not being unduly influenced by it

- Christians often compromise on the clarity of Scripture to avoid conflict.

- There are biblical reasons and times to be indignant, but even these can become sinful anger in a believer if not joined with love for others and the truth.

Reflection Questions

1. How would you respond to someone who says, "The Bible commands us not to judge anyone"?

2. How would you respond to someone who says Christianity only harms the world?

3. What is the difference between answering a question or challenge, and answering an individual?

Discussion Question

1. In what ways do you cultivate practical ways to represent truth with patient compassion? In what additional ways can you do so? Give specific examples of different settings in which you could cultivate these practices.

Quiz

1. According to Murray, Christians often struggle to be:
    a) In and of the culture
    b) In but not of the culture
    c) Isolated from culture
    d) Absent from culture

2. According to Murray, ___ out of ten Americans are practicing Christians.
    a) One
    b) Two
    c) Three
    d) Four

3. According to Murray, when Jesus said "do not judge," he was saying that when we judge, it is to be for the _____ of others, not their _____.

   a) Improvement, condemnation
   b) Condemnation, improvement
   c) Chastising, betterment
   d) None of the above

4. The problem with an unwelcoming and hostile spirit coming from Christians is that it:

   a) Provides a strong defense for the gospel but does not directly advance it
   b) Makes unbelievers follow the message of the gospel for the wrong reasons
   c) Ruins the credibility of the message based on the witness of the messenger
   d) Sets the focus of the message upon the messenger

5. According to Murray, those loud voices within the church that condemn "those people" outside the church often do so:

   a) Without reflecting on their own sins
   b) While acknowledging their own sins
   c) Without being heard
   d) According to their proper callings

6. On what does Murray base his exhortation regarding treating everyone with dignity, even those whom an individual may strongly disagree with?

   a) No one's mind can be changed through words
   b) Everyone is inherently good in their heart
   c) Everyone is a sinner in need of grace
   d) All of the above

7. Murray argues that if Christians are to contribute meaningfully to the cultural conversation through social media, they must do so with:

   a) Integrity
   b) Fear

    c) Indignation
    d) None of the above

8. According to Murray, the problem with the Pharisees was they sought to:

    a) Express love for people, but failed to love God
    b) Express love for God, but failed to love people
    c) Promote Jesus as the Messiah
    d) Interpret the law so as to earn them favor before Jesus

9. According to Murray, joining wise words and wise actions together:

    a) Gets things done
    b) Changes things
    c) Changes people
    d) All of the above

10. Murray reminds us that Paul suggested Christians respond to _____ when they encounter non-Christians.

    a) Controversies
    b) People
    c) Questions
    d) Political issues

CHAPTER 3

Confusion's Consequences–Getting Freedom Wrong

You Should Know

- Autonomy: belief that one is a law unto themselves and they determine what their reality is based on their perspective

- Gender neutral: the view that gender is a social construct and thus a person can decide to be whatever gender they desire

- Man is the measure of all things: phrase suggesting humanity's ability to master itself and the world

- Problems with gender-neutral language: denies a reality that God has made both male and female; runs contrary to languages that use gender-based systems for communication; hinders people from wrestling against feelings of gender dysphoria; creates a culture of fear of offense

- "I self-identify": a phrase used by someone to create a perceived reality in the hopes that a person will not offend them by denying that reality

- The sacrifices offered to human autonomy: 1) ability to reason; 2) moral accountability; 3) sense of human value; 4) freedom

- The Bible opposes unfettered autonomy and champions true freedom.

Reflection Questions

1. What is problematic about wanting to be free from being offended?

2. What does it mean to say "man is the measure of all things," and what is the problem with it?

3. How does the period of the judges and kings in Israel's history help shed light on current issues facing our society?

Discussion Question

1. How would you explain to someone the importance of maintaining freedom while opposing autonomy? What specific examples could you provide to someone of the difference between freedom and autonomy?

Quiz

1. According to Murray, the current climate, which prevents people from sharing ideas, has arisen because we have mistaken _____ for _____.

    a) Harmony, peace
    b) Love, freedom
    c) Identity, ideas
    d) Autonomy, freedom

2. Murray argues that freedom operates at its best within the confines of:

    a) Opinion
    b) Truth
    c) Personal preference
    d) Education

3. What is the result of unfettered autonomy?

    a) Everything becomes subject to personal preference
    b) Freedom is allowed in order that truth might be found

c) Everyone is given the ability to discover the truth

d) No one is hindered from expressing their feelings

4. According to Murray, the problem with autonomy is it does not just elevate personal preferences over truth, but it also:

a) Provides an alternative way for reason to be explored

b) Allows the pursuit of education to progress beyond previous boundaries

c) Fails to define what autonomy is

d) Elevates one's particular preference over another's

5. According to Murray, what key phrase tends to render as inoffensive a claim that something contrary to facts is true?

a) "The Bible says"

b) "No one knows"

c) "I self-identify"

d) "I feel"

6. Murray argues that de-gendering a language is:

a) Wise and good

b) Academic and propitious

c) Normal and advancing

d) Ethnocentric and imperialistic

7. The difference between humans and animals is that humans can:

a) Question and resist base drives

b) Immediately give in to base drives

c) Overcome facts

d) None of the above

8. How did humanity lose what it meant to be human and to value other human beings?

a) Humanity was placed a little lower than the angels

b) Humanity strove to become God rather than bear the image of God

c) Humanity sought to have dominion over the animals of the earth

d) Humanity wanted to know God better

9. Murray quotes Peter Singer as arguing that human babies can be killed because:

   a) It is unknown whether they will grow up to be of use to society
   b) The world's surplus population needs to be reduced
   c) They lack the mental capacity to value themselves
   d) Nothing is lost

10. According to Murray, our quest for autonomy is what:

   a) Frees us
   b) Enslaves us
   c) Empowers us
   d) Humbles us

CHAPTER 4

Clarity about Freedom

You Should Know

- Positive freedom: freedom that enables one to pursue excellence according to the ideals of what that excellence is

- Negative freedom: freedom from interference and constraint

- Truth: the foundation upon which freedom exists

- Determinism: the view that people do not have free will and live only according to chemical processes

- Inalienable rights: rights given by God by virtue of our being made in his image which can be violated by others, but never taken away

- Examples of positive freedom: 1) God giving the gift of sexuality to mankind but regulating it; 2) giving a child a yard to play in but keeping them from running into the street; 3) giving a child an allowance but not letting them spend it on harmful activities; 4) having the freedom to make money but not being allowed to steal from others

- Boundaries are necessary for preserving true freedom.

- Even secular humanists have become condemned by the post-truth confusion they have often cultivated.

Reflection Questions

1. What is the truth-and-freedom cycle?

2. How does Scripture affirm both negative and positive freedom?

3. What is necessary for people to truly have inalienable rights?

Discussion Question

1. If someone said there is no absolute standard of morality, how would you respond? What examples would you give from the world around you to defend your position? What scriptural proof would you provide to defend your position?

Quiz

1. What is the foundation of freedom?
    a) Autonomy
    b) Truth
    c) Education
    d) Peace

2. In John 8, Jesus claims to ___ the truth.
    a) Have
    b) Be
    c) Want
    d) None of the above

3. Negative freedom is:
    a) Freedom to explore nature
    b) Freedom from interference and constraint
    c) Freedom towards the people
    d) Freedom for excellence according to the ideals that define that excellence

4. Positive freedom is:
    a) Freedom to explore nature
    b) Freedom from interference and constraint
    c) Freedom towards the people
    d) Freedom for excellence according to the ideals that define that excellence

5. Which type of freedom is generally the one people, liberals and conservatives alike, define as freedom?

a) Positive freedom
b) Negative freedom
c) Neutral freedom
d) Neither

6. According to Murray, Western society tends to see restraints on our freedoms as:

a) Moral
b) Immoral
c) Harmless
d) Perceptive

7. Scripture sets up boundaries for our:

a) Punishment
b) Fulfillment
c) Enslavement
d) None of the above

8. Concerning inalienable rights, Murray argues that:

a) Rights may be violated but they cannot be taken away
b) Rights can be taken away
c) Rights are only good in so far as they are maintained
d) Nobody is born with rights

9. A failure to believe in human free will results in:

a) Determinism giving way to humanity's dark side
b) Determinism giving way to humanity's noble side
c) Truth being found inadvertently
d) Truth being found advertently

10. Jesus can set us free from our sins because:

a) We are worthy to be set free from those sins
b) We have minds that can come to an awareness of our sins
c) Others had failed to set us free
d) He has no sins of his own to be freed from

CHAPTER 5

Clarity about Human Dignity

You Should Know

- Golden Rule: the command of Jesus that we would do unto others as we would want them to do unto us

- Evil: a perversion of the good

- Human intentionality: not a naturally occurring phenomenon, but the product of design

- Instances where humanity is seen as the solution to its own problem: a Muslim believes that his good deeds must outweigh his bad deeds; an atheist believes he can better himself to avoid bringing suffering upon himself and others; a Buddhist believes she must free herself from all desire in order to enter into Nirvana

- Some paradoxes of the cross: justice and mercy are joined together; wrath and love are joined together; ugliness and beauty are joined together; unrighteousness and righteousness are joined together

- Many religions and philosophies have their own version of the Golden Rule.

- While everyone seems to agree with Jesus that humanity has a heart problem, everyone seems to resist the necessary truth that we need redemption through a source outside ourselves.

Reflection Questions

1. How would you respond to someone who said humans are just complex machines?

2. What would be an example of the contradiction we see in secularism of making us equal to God but less than human? How would you respond to this example?

3. What is the difference between the Golden Rule that Jesus gave and all other iterations of it from other ideologies?

Discussion Question

1. How does the cross show humans have dignity and worth? What are the implications for the daily lives of people?

Quiz

1. According to Murray, what is wrong with this statement: "Ethics is autonomous and situational, needing no theological or ideological sanction"?

    a) The statement is undefined

    b) The statement is written by only one individual

    c) The statement itself is an ideology

    d) The statement was never published

2. What is the problem with saying Europeans developed universal ethics?

    a) These ethics are not universal, as they were developed only by Europeans

    b) Their universals only apply for the generation that developed them

    c) The Europeans did not translate their propositions into other languages

    d) There is no problem

3. Some secular humanist neuroscientists suggest that our consciousness is explained purely by:

    a) The immortal soul

    b) A higher order

   c) The existence of God

   d) Neurons and brain chemistries

4. Murray argues that secular humanism inevitably leads to:

   a) Affirming human dignity based on a common consensus

   b) Directing one to an objective basis for dignity

   c) Believing human dignity is an illusion

   d) None of the above

5. According to Murray, if humans are just complex machines, then:

   a) There is a narrowing of scientific excellence

   b) All fields of study lose their meaning

   c) Greater clarity is brought to the study of the body

   d) All of the above

6. There are many scientific studies suggesting the mind:

   a) Is not the brain

   b) Is the brain

   c) Is a complex of chemicals

   d) Reacts only to external stimuli

7. If we are all inherently sinful, then we:

   a) Are beyond salvation

   b) Must make ourselves less sinful

   c) Cannot possibly save ourselves

   d) Can save ourselves

8. Evil is:

   a) Equal in power with good

   b) An eternal entity

   c) A perversion of the good

   d) All of the above

9. According to Murray, no greater respect is paid to human beings than:

   a) Our ability to reason

   b) Angels being sent to minister to humans

c) Our acknowledgment that we are evil
d) God being affected by our moral choices

10. Where is the infinite price for human dignity shown?

a) Creation
b) The fall
c) The cross
d) None of the above

CHAPTER 6

Clarity about Sexuality, Gender, and Identity

You Should Know

- Gnosticism: a heresy of the Christian faith that affirms that the body is evil and only pure soul or mind is good

- Objective standard: a fixed norm outside of ourselves by which we can judge whether something is right or wrong

- Diversity: ironically, the foundation for unity

- Sacred: something held in high regard by God and protected with boundaries

- What believers have in Christ: forgiveness of sins; a new identity; the comfort of Christ's presence through their suffering; a community of fellow sinners redeemed by Christ who bear one another's burdens

- Christianity affirms God made sexuality and gender good and sacred and put boundaries over them in order that a person might find true joy in them; forgiveness and healing are offered even to those who have violated those boundaries and have not followed God's will for sexuality and gender.

- Human sexuality can only be objectively sacred if its substance and expression do not depend on the vagaries of human opinion and perceived autonomy.

- Since the fall, everyone is dysphoric in some sense.

Reflection Questions

1. What makes discussing issues of sexuality and gender particularly confusing and heated?

2. What is the problem with determining morals based on the majority opinion of society?

3. What is the Christian view of the relationship between the mind and body?

Discussion Question

1. Briefly summarize why specific worldviews other than Christianity cannot account for a proper understanding of sexuality and maintain human dignity. How can believers stand resolute on biblical sexuality while both being aware of their own sinful tendencies in that area and showing compassion for others who need the redemptive and transforming power of Christ?

Quiz

1. Much of the confusion surrounding gender discussions is found in:
    a) Making a person a hero for announcing they are homosexual
    b) Everyone's refusal to talk about the issues
    c) A lack of charity shown towards those who disagree
    d) None of the above

2. Rather than making those who struggle with sexual identity into heroes, what ought to be given to them?
    a) The ability to determine whether or not they want to draw attention to their struggle
    b) Credibility before others
    c) The ultimate answers that they seek
    d) Whatever they wish

3. Why is denying that there is only male and female an injustice to those who have gender dysphoria?

   a) It does not allow them to find resolution to their struggle if they do not feel gender fluid
   b) It prevents the Bible from speaking into their lives
   c) They themselves might want to determine whether there are alternative ways to gender norms
   d) None of the above

4. Contrary to public opinion, the Bible, even with its limitations on sexual expression, is:

   a) Pro-expression
   b) Pro-love
   c) Pro-gender neutral
   d) Anti-love

5. Murray emphasizes that it is important, in discussions concerning homosexuality, to understand that:

   a) Homosexuality is a sin
   b) Every human alive is fractured in every way because of sin
   c) Every person has veered away from their originally intended purpose
   d) All of the above

6. According to Murray, what is needed in the debate over morally acceptable sexuality given the propensity for both sides to judge the other based on their own perceptions?

   a) A subjective standard
   b) An objective standard
   c) Agreement between both parties
   d) Another culture's perspective

7. Why is it problematic for naturalistic atheism to affirm homosexuality?

   a) It does not understand how people can have desires
   b) It robs people of free will to choose anything other than what they feel

c) It proposes that life's only purpose is to pass DNA through offspring
d) None of the above

8. According to Murray, God's boundaries on sex are for the sake of:
a) Protecting the sacredness of sexuality
b) Protecting people from confusion
c) Bringing order out of disorder
d) Preventing people from experiencing fulfillment

9. _____ considers the body to be corrupt or evil and the soul to be pure self.
a) Gnosticism
b) Christianity
c) Atheism
d) Islam

10. In Christ believers have:
a) A new identity
b) Solidarity with Christ in their suffering
c) A community of broken sinners to struggle alongside of
d) All of the above

CHAPTER 7

Clarity about Science and Faith

You Should Know

- Science: a method of observing, measuring, and making predictions about the physical world around us

- Faith: the assurance of things hoped for, the conviction of things not seen

- Vital question of faith: Is the person or thing we have faith in worthy of it?

- Scientism: a religious ideology that affirms science is either the only or the most reliable way to know the truth about the real world

- Some examples of what science can provide knowledge of include: that the universe had a beginning, the anatomy of a cell, the inner workings of the respiratory system, and how fast light travels

- The limitations of science include: it cannot determine what is right or wrong; it is only a tool; it cannot be a philosophical or religious worldview; it is limited to the physical senses; it is used by finite creatures who are limited in knowledge, life, and presence

- Science is a method of observing, measuring, and making predictions about the physical world.

- If contingent material things exist, then their existence must be explained by an immaterial noncontingent being.

Reflection Questions

1. What does it mean to suggest science does not "say" anything? What are the limitations of science?

2. Explain what biblical faith is.

3. What comfort can be found in knowing God made us and all things with intimate care?

Discussion Question

1. What is the relationship between faith and reason? How would you respond to someone who said you believe in God based on blind faith? Are there ways you could challenge them to see they too possess faith in something?

Quiz

1. If religion is rejected in favor of mere reason, then ethics:
   a) Are rooted in an objective standard
   b) Are transcendent
   c) Are subjective to mere opinion
   d) Are liberated

2. What example does Murray provide of a common narrative given in education to claim Christians are afraid of science?
   a) The discovery of fire
   b) The discovery of the laws of gravity
   c) The jailing of Galileo
   d) None of the above

3. ____ of scientists believe in a God who answers prayers.
   a) 1%
   b) 20%
   c) 25%
   d) 40%

4. What do proponents of scientism believe?

   a) Science is able to only answer questions through physical senses
   b) Science is the most reliable way to know truth about the real world
   c) Scientists should be the leaders of governments
   d) Science has an end goal in God

5. Naturalistic evolution entails that our beliefs are not based on whether they are true, but:

   a) Should be regarded as true nevertheless
   b) On how they help us survive and propagate our species
   c) Through faith in evolution, they are proven true
   d) On whether they are believed to be true

6. Darwinism _____ the Holocaust.

   a) Directly caused
   b) Delayed
   c) Did not directly cause, but influenced
   d) None of the above

7. Faith is:

   a) The evidence of things not seen
   b) Synonymous with hope
   c) A narrowing of one's perspective to a single point
   d) Our assurance and conviction of the things we do not see

8. According to Murray, the vital question of faith is:

   a) Does everyone have faith?
   b) Is the one we have faith in worthy of it?
   c) Can faith be proven?
   d) Who does not have faith?

9. Undeniable evidence:

   a) Cannot be proven
   b) Is an illusion
   c) Means people will always follow it
   d) Does not mean people will always follow it

10. What is the imagery Murray appeals to in Scripture to describe our creation? (pg. 182)

a) Built
b) Manufactured
c) Designed
d) Knitted

CHAPTER 8

Clarity about Religious Pluralism

You Should Know

- Exegesis: the act of interpreting a text wherein the person draws the interpretation out of the text

- Eisegesis: the act of interpreting a text wherein the person imposes an interpretation onto the text

- Tolerance operates best when differences are acknowledged and disagreements can be had.

- Exclusivism: the belief that some truths are exclusively true and all others are not

- Inclusivism: the belief that all beliefs are equally valid

- All-inclusivism contradicts itself.

- We currently think that challenging certain beliefs is the same thing as denigrating the person who holds them.

Reflection Questions

1. How would you respond to someone who said all religions lead to God?

2. Why is it problematic to say there is no proof of God, but faith is a rational choice based on personal experiences?

3. What elements are common to all religions and non-religious systems of thought? What makes Christianity fundamentally different from all other religions and non-religious faiths?

Discussion Question

1. What are the underlying motives for people wanting to believe in all-inclusivism? How does the gospel answer all the questions and desires of all religions and non-religions?

Quiz

1. Religious pluralism once meant:
    a) Only worldviews that were logically consistent could be affirmed in public
    b) All worldviews were to be accepted and affirmed since they are all equally valid
    c) No one had the right to persuade another that their belief was incorrect
    d) All worldviews could exist in the marketplace of ideas where their merits could be debated

2. Due to weariness with contentious religious debate, the public underwent a pendulum swing in order to:
    a) Maintain a forum for civil debate
    b) Avoid hurting anyone's feelings
    c) Convert everyone to one religion
    d) None of the above

3. Unless you _____, you cannot be a Buddhist. Unless you _____, you cannot be a Hindu.
    a) Do good works, abstain from good works
    b) Abstain from good works, do good works
    c) Affirm the divine self, deny self
    d) Deny self, affirm the divine self

4. Applying esoteric meanings to religious claims we do not prefer is _____.
    a) Ancient or an old way of interpreting the text
    b) Mythic or an analogical interpretation of the text

c) Exegesis or reading out of the text

d) Eisegesis or reading into the text

5. According to Murray, tolerance only operates among:

   a) Sameness, not differences
   b) Differences, not sameness
   c) Religions, not sciences
   d) Sciences, not religions

6. According to Murray, it is not possible to agree with everyone because:

   a) One would have to disagree with a person who claims that is false
   b) One must be well-versed in other religions
   c) No one can know everyone
   d) Agreement is a subjective standard

7. The problem with claiming to be all-inclusive is:

   a) It is all-inclusive
   b) It is only available to Hinduism
   c) It includes exclusivists
   d) It excludes exclusivists

8. Jesus is uniquely exclusive because he claims:

   a) To *have* the way
   b) To *discover* the way
   c) To *be* the way
   d) To *lead* the way

9. Nearly every other religion in some sense affirms a particular belief that Christianity claims is false. What is that belief?

   a) Humans cannot save themselves
   b) Humans can save themselves
   c) God created only physical matter
   d) God created only spiritual matter

10. In addition to the theological truths and real effects of the cross, what does it provide to humanity?

a) Unverifiable truth of Jesus's claims
b) Verifiable truth of Jesus's claims
c) Partial revelation of God's will
d) None of the above

CHAPTER 9

The Son through Fog: Clarity's Hope

You Should Know

- Biblical hope: a certainty in God's promises in Christ
- Secular hope: a desire that is uncertain of fulfillment
- John 8:32 (ESV): "You will know the truth, and the truth will set you free."
- The resurrection is important because it proved Jesus's claim that he would atone for sin, showed the value of humans and upheld our dignity, showed we are free from slavery to sin, proved we are free to be who we were intended to be.
- John 14:6 (ESV): "I am the way, and the truth, and the life. No one comes to the Father except through me."
- Autonomy in religion leaves a person uncertain and it takes away genuine freedom.
- It is inconsistent for an atheist to affirm objective morality and expect others to do the same.
- The resurrection of Jesus Christ vindicates his claims that he atoned for our sins.
- Post-truth culture provides only half the truth, which equals being all wrong.

Reflection Questions

1. What is biblical hope? How can it be said that Christianity is the foundation for hope in this world?

2. Why is truth irrelevant to naturalistic evolution, and how would you express that to someone who believed in it?

3. What does the resurrection of Jesus prove?

Discussion Question

1. Why do you believe in Jesus Christ, if you do? What things were particularly convincing to you in your decision to believe in Jesus or for maintaining your faith?

Quiz

1. What is the problem with secular hope?
   a) It is empirical
   b) It is rational
   c) It is calculated
   d) It is unsure

2. Where does autonomy ultimately lead in religion?
   a) It gives people freedom to believe what they want
   b) It preserves people from being offended
   c) It shows the unity all religions have with one another
   d) It turns against a religion that does not line up with it

3. What one thing makes our lives clear?
   a) We are rational beings
   b) We are made in God's image
   c) We are autonomous
   d) We have hope for a better future

4. Christendom's historical "black eyes" were due to:
   a) Islamic incursions
   b) An accurate following of Christianity
   c) The abuse of Christianity
   d) The threat of atheism

5. The three most common names given to girls in the Soviet Union, translated into English, were:

    a) Grace, Mercy, and Peace
    b) Strength, Endurance, and Patience
    c) Wonder, Sorrow, and Winter
    d) Faith, Hope, and Love

6. The worldview that influenced communist dictators was:
    a) Christianity
    b) Atheism
    c) Islam
    d) Gnosticism

7. Why doesn't God *need* humans in order to have relationship?
    a) Humans are incapable of having a relationship with God
    b) God needs humans for worship, but not to have a relationship with him
    c) The Father, Son, and Holy Spirit have an eternal relationship
    d) None of the above

8. According to Murray, in Jesus Christ:
    a) Only facts matter
    b) Truth and personal feelings converge
    c) Our personal feelings are taken away
    d) None of the above

9. According to Murray, what is wrong with the material trappings and experiences people have sought to fill themselves with?
    a) They lead only to wickedness
    b) They are neither true nor personal
    c) They fill only those who find them
    d) They are not equally valid for everyone

10. Who or what does Murray conclude is the Saving Truth?
    a) Jesus
    b) Man
    c) Reason
    d) Faith

Notes

www.ingramcontent.com/pod-product-compliance
Lightning Source LLC
Chambersburg PA
CBHW010038040426
42331CB00037B/3306